ROBOT SPORTS

DRONE RACING

Tom Jackson

Lerner Publications ◆ Minneapolis

TABLE OF CONTENTS

CHAPTER 1

IN THE ARENA

The lights go down in the arena, and everyone goes quiet. The race is about to begin! Suddenly, streaks of light begin to zoom around the center of the arena. These are the drones, and they are moving fast.

Drone racing is a new and exciting sport. It requires a lot of skill, and racers need to understand how the machines work. Racing drones can reach 90 miles (145 km) per hour! Fans can watch the world's best drone pilots in live online streaming events.

Many drone racing courses are set up outside.

Fast Facts

- Drone racers must pilot their drone around a course. The fastest wins.
- The racers wear headsets, with goggles, which display a live video stream from the drone.
- Some races are against the clock while others see four or more drones race against one another.

Each race is made up of several laps through a complex course. The drones have to pass through gates and around flags. The course is three-dimensional, so racers must zig-zag their drones from side to side as well as guide them up and down to complete each lap. Racers will normally get a chance to practice the course by themselves before the race begins.

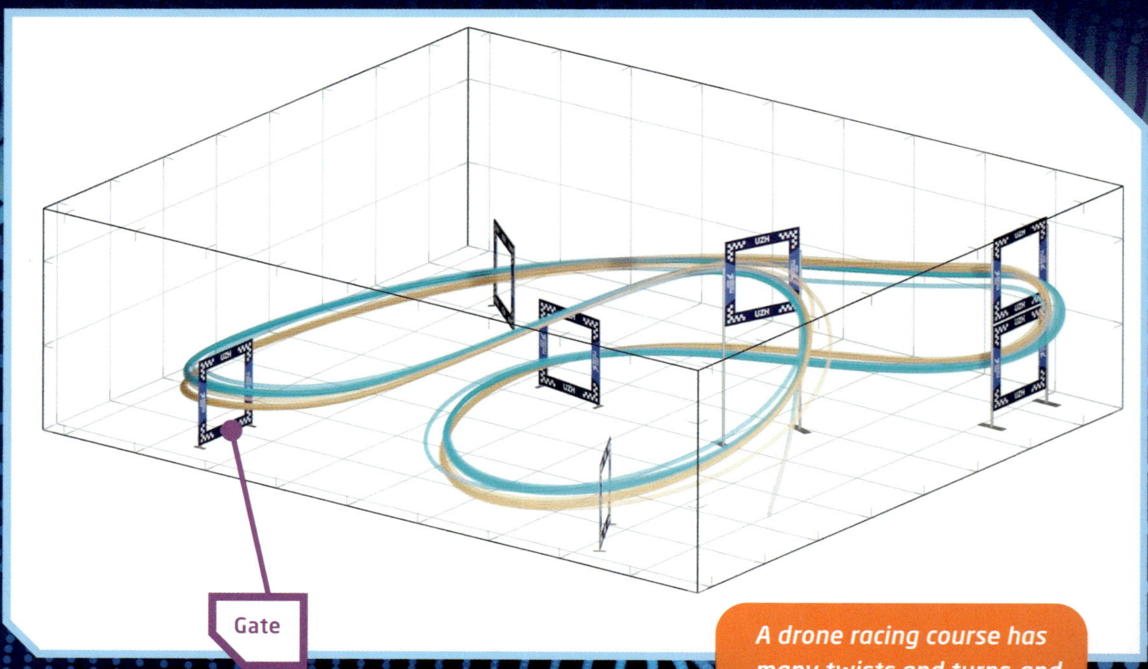

A drone racing course has many twists and turns-and ups and downs.

Alex Vanover is a world champion drone racer.

The drone pilot controls the drone remotely. They may be sitting near the course or in another room. They could be anywhere with a good Internet connection. Racers control drones using a first-person view (FPV). This means the screens in their goggles show what they would see if they were sitting inside the drone.

Drone racing is a new sport. The first official competitions started in 2014, with a race held inside a football stadium in Miami, Florida. The Drone Racing League, the world's largest drone racing group, was set up in 2015. However, FPV drone races were being held as early as 2011 in Germany and Australia.

Drones should be flown far away from other people and buildings.

An airplane makes a steep turn during an air race in Malaysia.

Before FPV drones became common, people raced with remote-controlled model airplanes. The pilots had to watch their model planes at all times to see where they were going. These races were similar to air races between full-sized, high-speed airplanes. There are still airplane races taking place around the world each year.

Modern drone races use quadcopters. These are small battery-powered aircraft that are very lightweight. They are powered by four spinning propellers. The propellers lift the drone into the air and help it hover in one place. The pilot uses a remote controller, or transmitter. The transmitter has joysticks and buttons to steer the drone and control its speed.

Video from the drone is sent back to the pilot's goggles.

TECH TALK

HOW A PROPELLER WORKS

A drone propeller has blades that spin around. As the propeller spins, the wing-shaped blades push the air down. The air pushes back in the opposite direction, so the drone rises. The drone can turn and move in any direction by adjusting the power to each propeller.

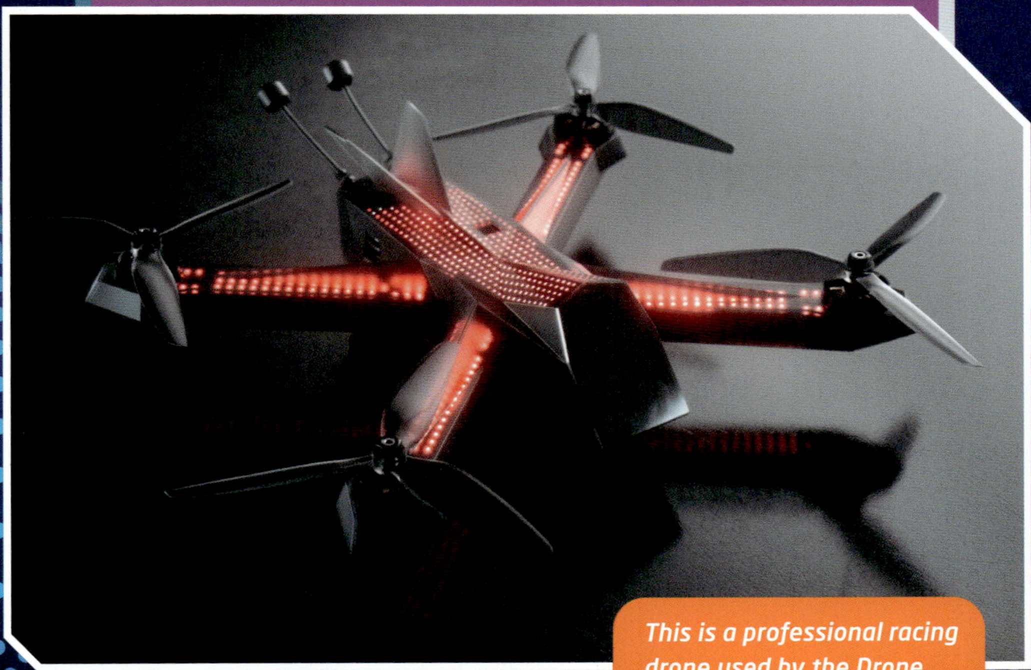

This is a professional racing drone used by the Drone Racing League.

CHAPTER 2

Race Time!

Let's get ready to race! There are several types of drone races, and each one has a different set of rules-and a different way to win!

It takes a lot of practice to learn the route around a course.

There are three main kinds of drone races: time trials, drag races, and rotorcross. The battery on a drone lasts for less than five minutes before it runs out of power. This means that drone races are short but always fast and exciting!

In a time trial, drones complete the course one at a time. The fastest time wins. The drone must fly through every gate along the course in the right order. If any are missed, the pilot has to turn around and go back.

A drag race is the same for drones as it is for cars. Several drones compete together. They fly in a straight line and speed up as quickly as they can. The winner is the drone that crosses the finish line first. As with all drone races, the drones begin the race lined up on a starting line with their motors off.

In a drag race, the pilot must stop the drone from flying off course.

This small drone is built to be easy to steer.

The US speed limit for drones is 100 miles (161 km) per hour. Most competitions set a top racing speed lower than that. Many drones are able to fly much faster. The highest speed ever reached for a quadcopter was 224 miles (361 km) per hour.

In a rotorcross race, several drones fly around the course at the same time. The number of competitors depends on the course. It is normally between three and six drones. The racers must overtake, block, and avoid hitting other drones as they fly around the course. Crashes are common, but the drones are very strong. Damaged parts are easy to replace.

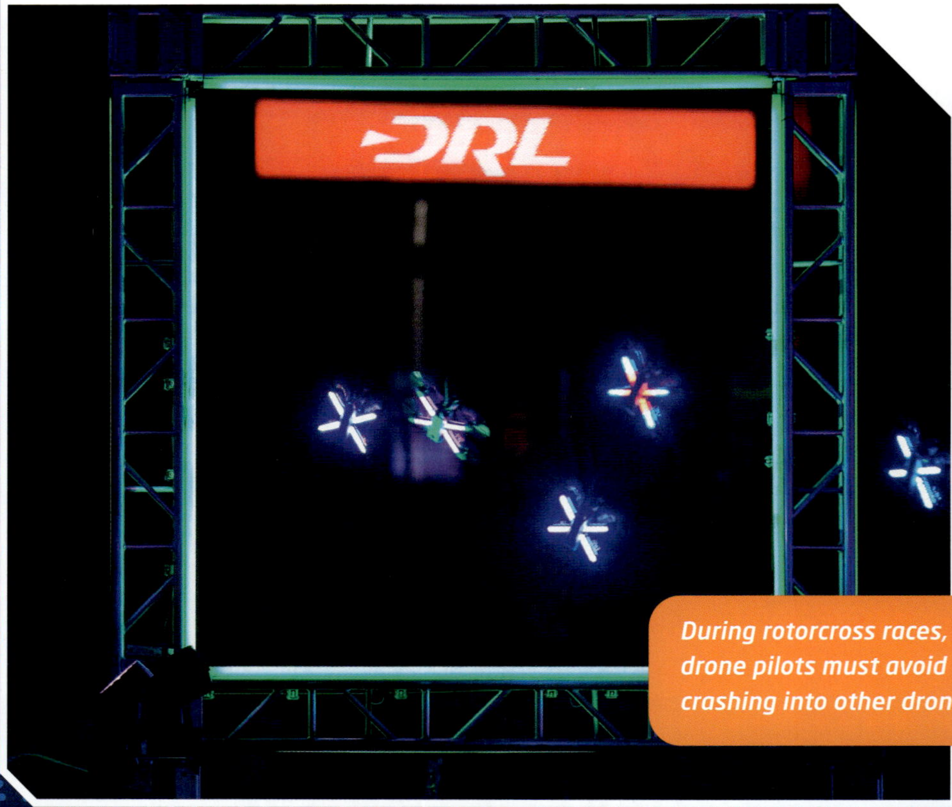

During rotorcross races, drone pilots must avoid crashing into other drones.

During a race, the pilot can only look at the course through the FPV goggles. This view only shows what is in front of the drone. In some events, a copilot can help by watching the course and warning the pilot if another drone is close behind.

TECH TALK

INSIDE FPV GOGGLES

The goggles have two small screens inside, one for each eye. Digital FPV goggles (*right*) create clear video. However, the digital signal takes longer to appear on the screens, so pilots may see what's happening too late and crash! Analog goggles are faster, but the video quality is not as good.

CHAPTER 3

HOW TO WIN

As well as being a skillful pilot, a successful drone racer needs to understand the technology used in the sport. If they get it right, they might become a world champion!

PARTS OF A DRONE

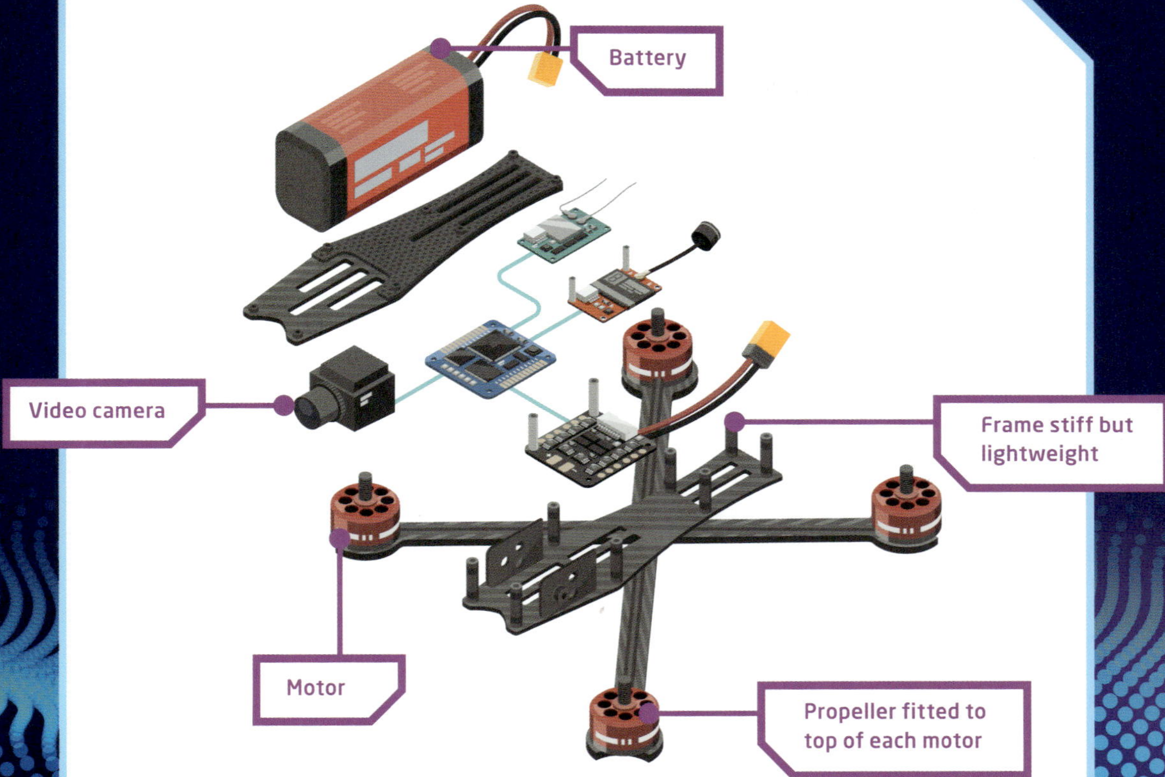

The big drone competitions, such as those run by the Drone Racing League, require all pilots to fly the same type of drone. That makes the races fair for all racers. However, amateur racers can make changes to their drones to give them an edge.

Drones use a lot of electricity, but the drone battery cannot be too big. That would make it heavy and would slow down the drone. One battery pack lasts between three and five minutes. It then takes about an hour to recharge. It is best to have several fully charged batteries ready to swap between flights. Professional drone pilots can use more than a hundred batteries a day!

Drones use up electricity fast. Pilots need a good supply of batteries.

Drone racers need a good tool kit to build and repair their drones.

The drone frame holds all the other parts in place. A professional racing drone is about 1 foot (30 cm) wide. This makes it big enough to carry powerful motors and a battery, but it is also small enough to be fast and easy to steer. The frame is made of carbon fiber. This is lightweight but tough. It does not break easily in crashes. The frame often has LED lights. They light up the drone so it is easier to see.

The World Air Sports Federation holds competitions for amateur racers around the world. However, the biggest races are held by the Drone Racing League (DRL). Pilots can qualify for championship races by competing in sim races. The sims run on game machines and computers. Anyone can join in.

Races always begin with the drones on the start line with their motors off.

DRL races are fast and exciting.

After qualifying, DRL pilots compete in races around the world. The pilots win points for completing a race. Only the best pilots get to fly in these races. They are shown on live television and streaming platforms. The pilot with the most points after a season of races is declared the champion. The best pilots share a prize of $100,000!

CHAPTER 4

DRONE SKILLS

There is more to flying drones than racing. The skills of a good drone pilot can be used in many other ways.

This incredible photo of a frozen forest was taken with a drone.

Racing drones are built for making fast turns. That makes them good for freestyle flying. A freestyler is not racing another pilot. They are just flying the drone to make exciting moves in the sky.

Other FPV drones are used for exploring remote places. They can capture amazing photos and video. These drones can stay in the air for longer than racing drones. They are also built to fly more smoothly. The pilots may use goggles to control these drones. They can also get a first-person view by watching a screen on the controller.

A firefighter prepares to fly a drone to get a better look at a dangerous fire.

Drones are very useful for search and rescue operations. They can be fitted with cameras that see heat instead of light. These cameras can locate people trapped under collapsed buildings or lost in the forest. The police also use drones to find people they are searching for.

In the future, more drones will use artificial intelligence (AI). AI is used in many drones, allowing them to work without a human controller. There are already AI drone racers that can take on the best human pilots. What do you think the future holds for drones and drone racing?

TECH TALK

VIRTUAL REALITY

The pilot of an FPV drone can only see forward. If they turn their head, their view stays the same. Adding cameras to the drone that look in all directions can create a virtual reality (VR) system. Wearing a VR headset, a drone pilot can look up, down, and behind to see everything around the drone.

A VR headset takes the wearer into a new world.

MEET A DRONE RACER

By the age of 18, Mincham Kim was already a two-time drone racing world champion. In 2023, Kim won the FAI World Air Sports Federation World Championship. He then became a pro racer for the DRL and won the championship in his first season. Kim began drone racing when he was 12. He practices for 12 hours every day!

YOUR TURN

Now that you know more about drone racing, it's time for you to get involved. The good news is anyone can do it. Here are some tips.

- Try being a drone pilot using a sim. There are several that run on computers and game consoles that use standard controllers.

- Search for a drone racing club near you. If there isn't one, you could set one up at your school.

- Watch professional racers in action. DRL events can be viewed on TV and streamed on the Internet.

GLOSSARY

amateur: someone who does something, like play a sport, for fun and is not paid

analog: based on continuous signals rather than digital number-based data

artificial intelligence (AI): a smart computer system

competitor: someone who takes part in a sport

course: the route followed by racers

propeller: a fan-shaped part that pushes air or water

quadcopter: a drone with four propellers

sim: short for *simulation*. An object or a place that is not real.

transmitter: the radio controller used for steering a drone

Learn More

Bolte, Mari. *Drones in Action*. Minneapolis: Lerner Publications, 2024.

Drones In School—How to Start a Team
https://www.dronesinschool.com/start-a-team

Drone Racing League—FPV 101
https://www.drl.io/fpv-101

Linde, Barbara M. *Drones for Racing and Sports*. New York: PowerKids Press, 2020.

Miller, Marie-Therese. *Speedy Drones*. Minneapolis: Lerner Publications, 2025.

Youth Drone Sports Championships
https://www.youthdronesports.org/

INDEX

PHOTO ACKNOWLEDGMENTS

Image credits: The Drone Racing League, pp. 4, 7, 16, 23, 28; Yanosh Nemesh/ Shutterstock, p. 5; www.nature.com/articles/s41586-023-06419-4/Wikimedia Commons, p. 6; Chai Koh Shin/Dreamstime.com, p. 8; CHEN WS/Shutterstock, p. 9; Erich Sacco/Shutterstock, p. 10; Dronelife.com, p. 11; Cloud System/Wikimedia Commons, p. 12; R3d Nemesis/Shutterstock, p. 13; Phatphum Phetchakan/Shutterstock, p. 14; Kietisak Yaemklebbua/Shutterstock, p. 15; tsyklon/Shutterstock, p. 17; Kite_rin/ Shutterstock, p. 18; Allahfoto/Shutterstock, p. 19; WINDCOLORS/Shutterstock, p. 20; Iurii Chornysh/ Shutterstock, p. 21; Travel Photos and Videos/Shutterstock, p. 22; Dmitry Kalinovsky/ Shutterstock, p. 24; marcin jucha/Shutterstock, p. 25; Mike Chapman/Shutterstock, p. 26; WESTOCK PRODUCTIONS/Shutterstock, p. 27; Juice Flair/Shutterstock, p. 29. Design elements: Rendix Alextian/Shutterstock, pp. 1, 3, 4, 12, 18, 24; Stocklekkies/ Shutterstock, pp. 5-11, 13-17, 19-23, 25-32.

Cover credits: Rendix Alextian/Shutterstock (top), Muhammad Javed/Dreamstime.com (top, centre); Stocklekkies/Shutterstock (middle); Markus Tretter/Dreamstime.com (bottom, left); Andrei Stepanov/Shutterstock (bottom, right).